Bryn Mawr Commentaries

Thucydides *Book VI*
Commentary

Cynthia W. Shelmerdine

Thomas Library, Bryn Mawr College
Bryn Mawr, Pennsylvania

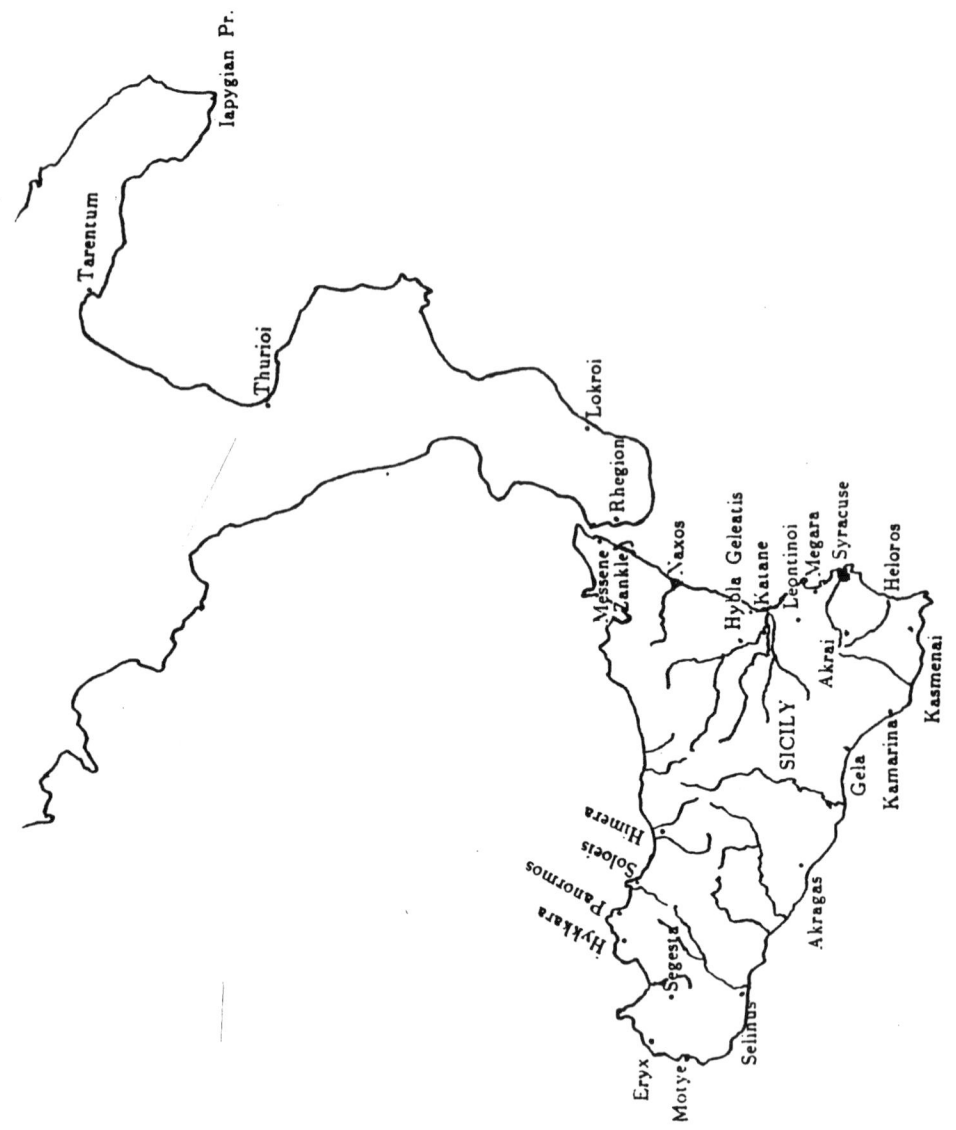

Copyright ©1989 by **Bryn Mawr Commentaries**

Manufactured in the United States of America
ISBN 0-929524-35-7
Printed and distributed by

Bryn Mawr Commentaries
Thomas Library
Bryn Mawr College
Bryn Mawr, PA 19010

Series Preface

These lexical and grammatical notes are meant not as a full-scale commentary but as a clear and concise aid to the beginning student. The editors have been told to resist their critical impulses and to say only what will help the student read the text. Our commentaries, then, are the beginning of the interpretive process, not the end.

We expect that the student will know the basic Attic declensions and conjugations, basic grammar (the common functions of cases and moods; the common types of clauses and conditions), and how to use a dictionary. In general we have tried to avoid duplication of material easily extractable from the lexicon, but we have included help with the odd verb forms, and recognizing that endless page-flipping can be counter-productive, we have provided the occasional bonus of assistance with uncommon vocabulary.

Production of these commentaries has been made possible by a generous grant from the Division of Education Programs, the National Endowment for the Humanities.

> Richard Hamilton, General Editor
> Gregory W. Dickerson, Associate Editor
> Gilbert Rose, Associate Editor

Introduction

This commentary is based on the Oxford Classical Text of Thucydides Book VI. Its aim is to provide help with grammar and translation, and thus to complement rather than to substitute for the fine commentary by K.J. Dover, *Thucydides Book VI, with an Introduction and Commentary* (Oxford 1965) [abbreviated 'D' throughout], which concentrates mainly on historical matters. Students are encouraged to use both, though I have incorporated or made reference to many of Dover's notes on translation, and have relied heavily on his work even where I have ventured to disagree with it. For helpful additions and corrections I am most grateful to the editors of *Bryn Mawr Commentaries* and their assistant Rebecca Ruttenberg; the responsibility for flaws which still remain is mine alone. I should also like to express my thanks to students at the University of Texas at Austin who used and improved this commentary in draft form. In addition to Dover I have usefully consulted the following:

T. Arnold, Θουκυδίδης. *The History of the Peloponnesian War, by Thucydides*, 2nd edition, vol. II (Oxford and London 1874)
J. Classen, *Thukydides*, revised by J. Steup, vol. 6 (Dublin and Zurich 1967)
J.D. Denniston, *The Greek Particles* (Oxford 1934)
A.W. Gomme, A. Andrewes and K.J. Dover, *A Historical Commentary on Thucydides*, vol. IV (Oxford 1970)
W.W. Goodwin, *Syntax of the Moods and Tenses of the Greek Verb* (Boston 1890)
C. Hude, *Scholia in Thucydidem* (Leipzig 1927)
B. Jowett, *Thucydides*, vols. I, II (Oxford 1881)
W.A. Lamberton, *The Sixth and Seventh Books of Thucydides* (New York 1886)
E.F. Poppo - J.M. Stahl, *Thucydidis de bello peloponnesiaco libri octo*, revised by J.M. Stahl, vol. III.2 (Leipzig 1880)
H.W. Smyth, *Greek Grammar*, revised by G.M. Messing (Cambridge, Mass. 1956) [abbreviated 'S' throughout].

Cynthia W. Shelmerdine
University of Texas at Austin

Commentary

1.1 τοῦ δ' αὐτοῦ χειμῶνος: genitive of time within which, "during the same winter." Thucydides narrates his history chronologically, dividing each year of the war into winter (November through mid-March) and summer (mid-March through October). χειμών here refers to the winter of 416/415 B.C. (the double designation is necessary for January to mid-March, when the Greek old year overlaps with our new year).
τῆς . . . Εὐρυμέδοντος: genitive of comparison, "(a force greater) than that (which went) with Laches and Eurymedon."
τῶν ἐνοικούντων . . . βαρβάρων: The word order shows where the emphasis is: "and, of the inhabitants, the number, both of Greeks and of foreigners."
καὶ ὅτι . . . Πελοποννησίους: parallel to μεγέθους and πλήθους, and like them governed by ἄπειροι.
οὐ πολλῷ τινί: "not by any great deal"; the simpler οὐ πολλῷ, "not by much," made indefinite.
ἀνῃροῦντο: imperfect middle of ἀναιρέω, "take up."
2 ὁλκάδι: a trading vessel, not a fast war ship.
τοσαύτη οὖσα: "although . . ."; one does not expect such a big island so close to the mainland.
ἐν: here, "by."
μάλιστα: with numbers, "about, approximately."
διείργεται τὸ μὴ ἤπειρος εἶναι: "it is prevented from being mainland." Verbs of preventing are usually followed by untranslated μή; the negative is μὴ οὔ.

2.1 ᾠκίσθη < οἰκίζω, "settle."
τὸ ἀρχαῖον: adverbial accusative, "in the beginning."
ὧδε, τοσάδε: referring to what follows, as usual.
τὰ ξύμπαντα: "in all." ξυ- = συ- throughout the History.
ἔχω + infinitive = "be able to."
ἀρκείτω: "let it suffice"; imperative of ἀρκέω.
εἴρηται: perfect passive of εἴρω (B); "it has been told," + dative of agent.
2 φαίνονται + participle = "are clear being x," i.e., "clearly are x"; whereas + infinitive would = "seem to be x."

1

καὶ πρότεροι: "even earlier" (D).
διὰ τὸ . . . εἶναι: articular infinitive, "on account of being."
ὑπὸ Λιγύων ἀναστάντες: ὑπό + genitive of personal agent gives an intransitive verb a passive meaning; "having been made to leave (ἀνίστημι) by the Ligurians."
τὰ πρὸς ἑσπέραν: adverbial, "in the parts toward the west."
3 Ἰλίου δὲ ἁλισκομένου: genitive absolute, "after Troy was captured"; present participle with perfect sense.
ἐκλήθησαν < καλέω.
Ἔγεστα: "Segesta."
προσξυνῴκησαν < προς-συν-οικέω, "join as additional settlers."
χειμῶνι: here, "by a storm."
κατενεχθέντες < καταφέρω; here, "bring ashore."
4 ὡς μὲν εἰκός: "as (is) reasonable."
τάχα . . . πως: "but perhaps (τάχα ἄν) also (καί) in some other way (ἄλλως πως)."
5 ἐλθόντες . . . στρατὸς πολύς: "having come . . . as a great army."
τὰ κράτιστα: here, "the best, richest (parts)."
ἐγγύς: with numbers, "about."
βορρᾶν: "North."
6 πλείω = πλείονα, neuter plural of πλείων, the comparative of πολύς.
Μοτύην . . . Πάνορμον: objects of ἐνέμοντο.
ὅτι: here, "because."
ἐλάχιστον πλοῦν: accusative of extent of space.
Καρχηδών: Carthage.
3.1 Χαλκιδῆς = Χαλκιδεῖς, nominative plural, "Chalcidians."
Θουκλέους: genitive sing. of Θουκλῆς, "Thukles."
ὅταν . . . πλέωσι: present general, "whenever they sail . . ."
2 Συρακούσας: Syracuse, like Athens, is a feminine plural city name.
τοῦ ἐχομένου ἔτους: "the following year" (D).
ἐξελάσας: aorist active participle of ἐξελαύνω.
νῦν οὐκέτι περικλυζομένῃ: "now no longer washed all around," i.e., "no longer an island." The "inner city," Ortygia, was connected to the mainland by the sixth century B.C. (D).
3 μετὰ Συρακούσας οἰκισθείσας: lit., "after Syracuse having been founded," i.e., "after Syracuse had been founded."
Λεοντίνους: Leontinoi, a masculine plural city name.

4.1 κατά: "about," as often in expressions of time.
Μεγάρων: Megara, a neuter plural city name.
ὑπέρ: "beyond," + genitive.
ὄνομα: "by name."
αὐτόθεν: "from here." -θεν signifies place from which; -δε, place to which.
ὀλίγον χρόνον: "for a little while"; accusative of duration of time.
ὑπὸ αὐτῶν ἐκπεσών: "having been driven out by them" (see on ὑπὸ Λιγύων ἀναστάντες, 2.2). ἐκπίπτω is used as the passive of ἐκβάλλω.
Ὕβλωνος ... προδόντος ... καὶ καθηγησαμένου: genitive absolute, "since Hyblon...."
Μεγαρέας ... Ὑβλαίους κληθέντας: "the Megarians called Hyblaean"; an ethnic used as a place indication.
2 αὐτοὺς οἰκίσαι: "after founding it (Μεγαρέας Ὑβλαίους)"; not, as D translates, "Megara itself."
καὶ ἐκ Μεγάρων ... ξυγκατῴκισεν: See D for the textual problem here.
3 Γέλα: (Doric) genitive singular of Γέλας, "Gela."
οὗ: "where."
νόμιμα: "institutions" (D).
ἐτέθη < τίθημι.
4 ἐγγύτατα: See on ἐγγύς, 2.5.
5 τὴν μὲν ἀρχήν: adverbial accusative, "at first."
Ὀπικίᾳ: Southern Italy.
καί ἀπὸ Χαλκίδος καὶ ... Εὐβοίας: "also from Chalcis and ... Euboea."
ξυγκατενείμαντο: plural to go with plural sense of subject πλῆθος.
τὴν ἰδέαν: accusative of respect with δρεπανοειδές, "sickle-shaped in its form."
ἐκπίπτουσι: See on ὑπὸ αὐτῶν ἐκπεσών, 4.1.
προσέβαλον: here, "put in at" + dative.
6 ἀνθρώπων: genitive of material, "with men."
τὸ ἀρχαῖον: See on 2.1.
5.1 Χαλκιδῆς ... οἱ πλεῖστοι: "Chalcidians the majority," i.e., most were Chalcidians. οἱ πλεῖστοι Χαλκιδῆς would = "most of the Chalcidians."
ἐκράθη < κεράννυμι, "mix."
3 λύτρα: "as ransom (for, + genitive)," in apposition to τὴν γῆν in the next line.

ἀνάστατος: fem.; many compound adjectives have only two terminations (masculine/feminine and neuter).

6.1 ὥρμηντο: pluperfect middle of ὁρμάω; "they had urged themselves on, rushed," i.e., "they were eager."
τῆς πάσης: sc. of Sicily; genitive with ἄρξαι.
ξυγγενέσι . . . ξυμμάχοις: datives with βοηθεῖν.

2 [τε]: Square brackets enclose material the editor thinks is intrusive.
προθυμότερον: comparative adverb, here intensive; "eagerly" (S 1067).
καθέστασαν: pluperfect active (intransitive) of καθίστημι, "come into a (certain) state," here, a state of war.
γαμικῶν τινῶν: "questions of marriage" (Jowett).
ξυμμάχους: "as allies."
αὐτούς: the Segestans.
τὴν γενομένην: The noun is ξυμμαχίαν in line 12.
ἐπὶ + genitive = "in the time of."
οἱ Ἐγεσταῖοι: artfully placed inside "alliance . . . with Leontinoi," though properly belonging outside, both grammatically and politically.
ἀναμιμνῄσκοντες: "reminding x (accusative) of y (accusative)."
ἐδέοντο: imperfect, "kept on asking them."
σφίσι: "them," i.e., the Segestans; object of ἐπαμῦναι.
λέγοντες . . . εἶναι: The protasis of this condition is future most vivid (S 2328), with future indicative verb; the verb in the apodosis is εἶναι, an infinitive in indirect discourse depending on λέγοντες.
κεφάλαιον: "chiefly," or "in sum."
ξυμμάχους αὐτῶν: i.e., allies of Athens (D).
σχήσουσι: ἔχω has two future tenses. ἕξω (from present stem) expresses an ongoing process, "I will (go on) hav(ing)"; σχήσω (from aorist stem) expresses a single act, "I will acquire (and then have)."
μὴ . . . ξυγκαθέλωσιν < ξυν-κατα-αἱρέω; clause of fearing after an expression of apprehension (κίνδυνον εἶναι). Though optative is expected after a past tense (ἐδέοντο), the subjunctive is used for vividness.
Δωριεῦσι . . . Πελοποννησίοις: datives with βοηθήσαντες.
καὶ τὴν . . . δύναμιν: "their (the Athenians') power also," i.e., as well as that of Sicily.
σῶφρον δ' εἶναι: governed by λέγοντες in line 13.

ἄλλως τε καί: "both otherwise and," i.e., especially. Here followed by genitive absolute.
σφῶν: i.e., the Segestans.
3 σκεψομένους, εἰσομένους (< *εἴδω): future participles expressing purpose.
περί τε ... ὑπάρχει: "to see if the money is there." The subject is placed before its clause (prolepsis, S 2182).
τῷ κοινῷ: the public treasury.
ὅτῳ = ᾧτινι, "in what (state)."
7.1 ἀπεστάλησαν: aorist passive of ἀποστέλλω.
ἔτεμον: The winter wheat would be sufficiently high to be cut down.
τῆς ἄλλης: "the rest of."
σπεισάμενοι < σπένδω, "pour (libations)"; in middle, "pour libations with one another," hence "make a truce, treaty."
τὴν ἀλλήλων: sc. γῆν, χώραν, as often in Thucydides.
τῷ στρατῷ: "with (their) army."
2 ὑπὸ δὲ νύκτα: "at night"; with ἐκδιδράσκουσιν.
ἄπωθεν: "far off."
τῇ ὑστεραίᾳ: sc. ἡμέρᾳ; dative of time at which something is done.
ᾔσθοντο < αἰσθάνομαι.
3 σφῶν τε αὐτῶν: with ἱππέας, correlated with Μακεδόνων ... φυγάδας.
4 παρὰ Χαλκιδέας: "to the Chalcidians"; παρά often for πρός when the object is a person rather than a place.
ἄγοντας ... σπονδάς: "observing/keeping truces."
8.1 τοῦ δ' ἐπιγιγνομένου θέρους: "during the following summer," i.e., 415 B.C.; see on 1.1.
ἅμα ἦρι: "together with," i.e., "at the beginning of spring."
ἀσήμου ἀργυρίου: uncoined silver, bullion.
ὡς ... μηνὸς μισθόν: "as a month's wage."
2 ἀκούσαντες: ἀκούω = "hear x (accusative) from person y (genitive)."
τά τε ἄλλα ... χρημάτων: "both other tempting (i.e., persuasive) and false arguments, and (in particular) about the money."
τὸν Κλεινίου: standard formula for "the (son) of Kleinias."
βοηθούς: sc. εἶναι, parallel to ξυγκατοικίσαι.
ἤν (= ἐάν) τι ... πολέμου: See D.
3 ἡμέρᾳ πέμπτῃ: "on the fourth day"; Greek counting is inclusive.

6   Thucydides Book VI

καθ' ὅτι χρή: "concerning in what way it is right" (lit., "according to what . . .").
γίγνεσθαι: used as passive of middle ποιεῖσθαι, as usual.
τοῦ = τινος, genitive with προσδέοιντο.

4 ᾐρημένος < αἱρέω.
ἐφίεσθαι: + genitive, as usual with "desire."
παρῄνει < παραινέω, "advise."

9.1 ξυνελέγη: "assembled, came together"; aorist passive of συλλέγω, with active meaning.
αὐτοῦ τούτου: "this very thing."
μὴ . . . ἄρασθαι: "not to take upon ourselves"; aorist middle infinitive of αἴρω. Infinitive after χρῆναι, not σκέψασθαι.
βραχείᾳ βουλῇ: "short (i.e., insufficient) deliberation."
πόλεμον οὐ προσήκοντα: "a war that has nothing to do with (us)," i.e., is none of our business.

2 ἔγωγε καί: emphatic; "I, for my part, even."
τοῦ τοιούτου: i.e., making war.
νομίζων: "although I think."
ὁμοίως: i.e., as good as one who (like Nicias) does not concern himself about his life and property.
τι: with προνοῆται; "takes any thought for," + genitive.
δι' ἑαυτόν: "for his own sake."
παρὰ γνώμην: "contrary to (my) opinion/thought."
ᾗ ἄν: "in whatever way."

3 πρός: "considering."
τοῖς ἑτοίμοις: dative of respect, with κινδυνεύειν; "put at risk/run risks with what is at hand."
ὡς = ὅτι, "that."
κατασχεῖν: aorist of κατέχω.

10.1 καὶ ἑτέρους: "others as well."

2 ὀνόματι: "(only) in name"; explained by the parenthesis which follows.
οὕτω: sc. in name only.
ἐνθένδε: "from here (Athens)"; sc. opponents of the treaty; balanced by ἐκ τῶν ἐναντίων.
σφαλέντων . . . δυνάμει: "but if we suffer defeat anywhere with a significant force."
ταχεῖαν . . . ἐπιχείρησιν: not "a swift attack," but "an attack which will be swift"; note article and its position.
οἷς . . . ἡ ξύμβασις . . . ἐγένετο: "for whom the treaty was made"; see on γίγνεσθαι, 8.3.

πρῶτον μέν: the first reason why the treaty will not prevent an attack; answered by ἔπειτα in line 7.
διὰ ξυμφορῶν: "as a result of disasters."
ἐκ τοῦ αἰσχίονος ἢ ἡμῖν: "from a position more shameful (for them) than for us."
αὐτῇ ταύτῃ: "this very (treaty)."
πολλὰ . . . ἔχομεν: "the disputed points which we have are many"; note article.

3 εἰσὶ δ' οἵ: "there are (people) who," i.e., "some people."
διὰ τὸ . . . ἡσυχάζειν: articular infinitive; see on διὰ τὸ . . . εἶναι, 2.2.
καὶ αὐτοί: "they themselves too," just like the Spartans. The nominative of αὐτός is always intensive.

4 δίχα: adverbial, "divided."
καὶ πάνυ: "by all means."
ξυνεπιθοῖντο < ξυν-επι-τίθημι, "attack jointly, join in attacking." For the optative in -θοῖντο instead of -θεῖντο see S 746c.
πρὸ πολλῶν ἂν ἐτιμήσαντο: i.e., would have valued highly.

5 τινά: indefinite pronoun, subject of σκοπεῖν.
<τῇ>: Angle brackets enclose material supplied by the editor.
ἀρχῆς: genitive with verb of desire (ὀρέγεσθαι, "strive for").
ἀφεστῶτες: perfect active (intransitive) participle of ἀφίστημι.
ἐνδοιαστῶς ἀκροῶνται: "listen doubtfully," < ἀκροάομαι.
ὡς ἀδικουμένοις: ὡς + participle = "because, on the grounds that . . ."
μέλλομεν ἀμύνεσθαι: "we delay punishment."

11.1 τοὺς μέν: "the latter," i.e., the unruly allies; τῶν δέ, "the former," are the Sicilians.
κἄν: καί = "also."
εἰ καί: "even if."
διὰ πολλοῦ . . . ὄντων: genitive absolute, "since they are far away and many."
ἀνόητον: sc. ἐστι.
ὧν: genitive with verb of ruling (κρατήσας), "whom (even) if one conquers (them)."
ἐν τῷ ὁμοίῳ καί: "in the same (position) as."

2 ἄν . . . γενέσθαι: "that they would be."
ὅπερ: "with/about which very (thing)."

3 νῦν μέν: "as it is, in the current circumstances"; answered by ἐκείνως δ᾽, "in that case" (i.e., if Syracuse ruled them).
Λακεδαιμονίων . . . χάριτι: "out of friendship to the Spartans."
οὐκ εἰκός: sc. ἐστι, "it is not likely."
τὴν ἡμετέραν: sc. ἀρχήν.
ὧν αὐτῶν: the Peloponnesians.
οὗ αὐτοῦ: sc. τρόπου.
μᾶς δ᾽ ἄν . . . ἐκπεπληγμένοι εἶεν: "they would be terrified f us"; < ἐκπλήσσω.
:εἶ: in Sicily.
᾽ ὀλίγου: "after a short (time)" (D).
ὰ διὰ πλείστου: "the things farthest away"; cf. διὰ πολλοῦ . . . ὄντων, 11.1.
πεῖραν . . . τῆς δόξης: "opportunity to test their reputation."
σφαλείημεν: aorist passive opt. of σφάλλω, "trip up."
ὑπεριδόντες: "looking down on (us)."
μετὰ τῶν ἐνθάδε: "with our (enemies) here."
ἐπιθοῖντο: See on 10.4.
5 διὰ τὸ . . . περιγεγενῆσθαι: "because you have overcome them against expectation, compared with (πρός) what you feared at first."
6 μηδὲ Λακεδαιμονίους . . . θήσονται: i.e., (χρὴ) μηδὲ ἡγήσασθαι Λακεδαιμονίους ἄλλο τι σκοπεῖν ἤ, διὰ τὸ αἰσχρόν, ὅτῳ (= ᾧτινι) τρόπῳ ἔτι καὶ νῦν εὖ θήσονται τὸ σφέτερον ἀπρεπές (= ἀπρέπειαν), ἤν (= ἐὰν) δύνωνται, σφήλαντες ἡμᾶς.
ὅσῳ καί: "to the extent that."
περὶ πλείστου καὶ διὰ πλείστου: "to the greatest (degree) and for the longest (time)."
7 οὐ . . . ὁ ἀγών: sc. ἐστι.
ὅπως: "how," with future (φυλαξόμεθα, here "guard against") in an object clause after a verb of effort (S 2209).
12.1 βραχύ τι: adverbial, "a bit, slightly."
λελωφήκαμεν < λωφάω, "have a respite from."
ηὐξῆσθαι: perfect middle/passive infinitive of αὐξάνω, "grow, increase."
εἶναι: Omit, with ms. C. If retained, it must be governed by μεμνῆσθαι χρή ("it is right to remember that it is just . . .") or by ὥστε.
ἀναλοῦν < ἀναλόω, rare form of ἀναλίσκω, "use up, spend."
οἷς . . . χρήσιμον: "(fugitives) to whom (it is) advantageous to lie well."

καὶ τῷ ... κινδύνῳ: instrumental dative; "through danger to the man nearby," i.e., to someone else. The καί connects ψεύσασθαι with ἢ εἰδέναι and ἢ ξυναπολέσαι.
αὐτοὺς ... παρασχομένους: "themselves supplying only words."
χάριν ... εἰδέναι: "do not feel properly grateful."

2 ἄσμενος αἱρεθείς: "delighted at having been chosen."
τὸ ἑαυτοῦ: "his own aim/advantage."
ἄλλως τε καί: See on 6.2.
νεώτερος: "too young."
δέ ... καί: "and ... also."
μηδὲ τούτῳ ἐμπαράσχητε: imperative, "do not empower this man."
ἰδίᾳ: adverbial, "privately, on his own account."
μὴ οἷον νεωτέρῳ· "not the sort of thing for a young man to ..."

13.1 Οὕς: "these (sorts of men)"; a relative at the beginning of a sentence is often demonstrative.
τῳ = τινι, with τῶνδε.
ὅπως μή: "lest," with future after verbs of fear and caution (S 2231).
μηδ' ... δυσέρωτας εἶναι: governed by ἀντιπαρακελεύομαι.
ἐλάχιστα: can be taken as subject of κατορθοῦνται, despite plural verb; see D.
ὡς ... κίνδυνον ἀναρριπτούσης: "on the grounds that it is running a risk."
ἀντιχειροτονεῖν: governed by ἀντιπαρακελεύομαι.
οἷσπερ νῦν: "the very ones which now (are used/observed)," i.e., "the same ones as now."
χρωμένους: "using," i.e., "observing" + dative.
ξυμφέρεσθαι: "settle their differences, come to terms."

2 ξυνῆψαν ... πόλεμον: "engaged in war," < ξυνάπτω.
τὸ λοιπόν: "for the future."
ποιεῖσθαι: Understand ἡμᾶς as subject.
τευξόμεθα < τυγχάνω.

14.1 γνώμας προτίθει αὖθις: "put forward the proposal again."
ἀναψηφίσαι: "put to a second vote" (D).
λύειν τοὺς νόμους: See D.
τὸ καλῶς ... βλάψῃ: The switch from articular infinitive to relative clause is awkward; "ruling well is this, whoever benefits ... ," i.e., "ruling well is benefitting."
ὡς πλεῖστα: "as much as possible."

ἑκὼν εἶναι: adverbial, "willingly" (S 2012c).
15.1 τῶν δὲ Ἀθηναίων ... ἀντέλεγον: See D.
2 βουλόμενος τῷ τε: balances καὶ μάλιστα ... ἐπιθυμῶν. For postponed τε see D's introduction, I.3.15(a).
ὧν ... καὶ ὅτι: "because he was ... and because ..."
τὰ πολιτικά: accusative of respect; not to be joined with τἆλλα.
ἐμνήσθη: "mentioned," < μιμνήσκομαι, + genitive.
δι' αὐτοῦ: "through this office," i.e., = διὰ τοῦ στρατηγεῖν. Probably not "through him," since Alcibiades is the subject of λήψεσθαι (< λαμβάνω) (see D).
τὰ ἴδια: object of ὠφελήσειν.
3 καθεῖλεν < καθαιρέω.
4 αὐτοῦ: with μεγέθος τῆς ... παρανομίας ... καὶ τῆς διανοίας.
τῆς διανοίας ... ἔπρασσεν: See D.
καθέστασαν: See on 6.2.
διαθέντι: sc. αὐτῷ; with ἀχθεσθέντες.
οὐ διὰ μακροῦ: "after not much time, in a short space of time."
16.1 καὶ προσήκει μοι ... καὶ ἄξιος ...: "both ... and ..."
ἄρχειν: here = "rule," but ἄρξασθαι = "begin."
καθήψατο < καθάπτομαι, "attack."
ὧν ... πέρι = περὶ ὧν; the accent is shifted when the preposition is postpositive (anastrophe, S 175a).
2 καὶ ... μείζω: "greater even beyond its (actual) power."
τῷ ἐμῷ διαπρεπεῖ: "because of my eminence"; see D's introduction, I.3.8.
ἐλπίζοντες: "expecting," as often.
καθῆκα: here, "sent down (into the arena), entered (for racing)"; < καθίημι.
τιμὴ τὰ τοιαῦτα: When only one of two nouns in the nominative has an article, it is the subject and the other is the predicate (S 1150).
3 φθονεῖται: "they (ὅσα) provoke envy."
ᾗδ' ἡ ἄνοια, ὃς ἄν: See on τὸ καλῶς ... βλάψῃ, 14.1.
τοῖς ἰδίοις τέλεσι: "by his private means, at his own expense."
4 ἄδικον: sc. ἐστιν.
πρὸς ... ἰσομοιρεῖ: "has an equal share of misfortune with no one."
δυστυχοῦντες οὐ προσαγορευόμεθα: "we are not greeted when we are down on our luck."

ἀνεχέσθω: 3rd singular imperative, "let (a man) hold out, bear up."
τὰ ἴσα νέμων: "giving equal treatment," to fortunate and unfortunate alike.
5 ὄντας: οἶδα takes accusative + participle in indirect discourse.
τῶν δὲ ἔπειτα ἀνθρώπων: "the men of future generations"; genitive with τισί in next line.
ταύτῃ αὔχησιν: with καταλιπόντας; "having left behind for this (homeland) a boast."
6 ὧν: i.e., this kind of fame (D).
τὰ ἴδια ἐπιβοώμενος: "although I am criticized (lit., cried out against) for my private actions."
τὰ δυνατώτατα: "the most powerful (elements)."
Λακεδαιμονίους . . . κατέστησα . . . ἀγωνίσασθαι: "I made the Spartans fight."
ἐς μίαν ἡμέραν: "within one day."
καὶ περιγενόμενοι: "even though they prevailed."
17.1 καὶ ταῦτα . . . ἔπεισεν: "and (of) this my youth and what seemed my unnatural folly regarding the area of Spartan control hit upon the appropriate words and persuaded (them), offering in its spirit a guarantee."
πεφόβησθε: perfect middle imperative with present sense.
ἀποχρήσασθε: "make full use of"; the prefix intensifies.
3 τὰ . . . σῶμα, τὰ . . . χώρᾳ: accusatives of respect.
ἐξήρτυται: perfect middle/passive of ἐξαρτύω, "fit out, equip with" + dative.
νομίμοις κατασκευαῖς: "farms of the usual kind" (D).
ὅτι: neuter indefinite relative pronoun, object of λαβών in next line. The overall structure is ὅτι λαβὼν οἴεται ἄλλην γῆν οἰκήσειν, ταῦτα ἑτοιμάζεται.
ἐκ τοῦ . . . πείθειν: lit., "from persuading by speaking," explaining λαβών, as does στασιάζων.
τοῦ κοινοῦ: See on 6.3.
5 ἐκείνοις: sc. εἰσίν; dative of possession.
διεφάνησαν . . . ὄντες: "turned out to be."
αὐτοὺς ἐψευσμένη: "having been mistaken about them (hoplites)," i.e., about how many there were, or (middle) "having falsely represented them," i.e., as being more numerous than they were.
6 τοιαῦτα: i.e., equally εὔπορα.
αὐτοῖς: "ourselves."

7 τοὺς αὐτοὺς... πλεῖν: "these same enemies whom they say we, now leaving behind, would sail," i.e., "whom we would leave behind now if we made the expedition."
8 οὔτε ἀνέλπιστοι ... εἴ τε καί: "the Peloponnesians were never more without hope as regards us, and even if..."
οὔτε and εἴ τε are correlative.
ἔρρωνται: perfect passive of ῥώννυμι with present sense, "have strength."
τὸ ... ἐσβάλλειν: articular infinitive with ἱκανοί εἰσι, "they are sufficient (in number) for invading."
ὑπόλοιπον ... ναυτικόν: the navy that would remain in Athens if they *did* sail to Sicily.

18.1 καὶ μὴ ... ἐκεῖνοι ἡμῖν: See Nicias' argument at 13.2.
2 φυλοκρινοῖεν ... βοηθεῖν: "should choose by race those whom they ought to help."
βραχὺ ... αὐτῇ: "adding (only) a little to it," i.e., to their ἀρχή.
ἔπεισι < ἔπειμι, "will attack"; future indicative with ὅπως after a verb of effort (S 2211).
3 οὐκ ἔστιν: "there is no way, it is not possible."
ἐς ὅσον: "the extent to which."
ἀνιέναι < ἀνίημι, "let go."
διὰ τὸ ... κίνδυνον εἶναι: τὸ εἶναι is the articular infinitive here; "because there is a danger to ourselves (αὐτοῖς) that we would be ruled (ἀρχθῆναι ἄν, future less vivid condition) by others."
ἐκ τοῦ αὐτοῦ ... ἥσυχον: "you must not consider quietness on the same (terms) as others"; ἐπισκεπτέον is verbal adjective modifying τὸ ἥσυχον, with dative of agent.
4 ποιώμεθα: hortatory subjunctive (S 1797); "let us..."
εἰ δόξομεν: See D.
τῶν ἐκεῖ προσγενομένων: genitive absolute, "the things having been added on," i.e., "with the addition of the territory there."
ἐν ᾧ: "in which (case)."
5 καὶ μένειν ... καὶ ἀπελθεῖν: with τὸ ἀσφαλές, "safety, both for staying and for departing" (D).
6 μὴ ... ἀποτρέψῃ: prohibition (S 1800b, 1840C N.), "let not..."
ἐς τάδε ἦραν αὐτά: "raised (the empire) to this (height)."
ἄν ... ἄν: The first ἄν simply anticipates the second and is not translated (S 1765).

ξυγκραθέν < ξυγκεράννυμι, "mixed together."
τρίψεσθαι . . . αὐτήν: "wear herself out on herself."
τὸ ἀμύνεσθαι . . . ξύνηθες ἕξειν: "will have defending itself as customary," i.e., "will be used to defending itself."
7 ἀπραγμοσύνης μεταβολῇ: "by a change to inactivity" (D).
20.1 ξυνενέγκοι . . . βουλόμεθα: "may these things turn out (< ξυμφέρω) as we want."
σημανῶ: future of σημαίνω.
2 ῥᾴω = ῥᾴονα, masculine/feminine accusative singular comparative of ῥᾴδιος.
ἂν . . . προσδεξαμένας: potential participle, "(ones) who would receive."
τό τε πλῆθος . . . Ἑλληνίδας: "and in number, the Greek cities (are) many for one island."
4 ἐστὶ Σελινουντίοις: dative of possession; "the Selinuntians have."
κέκτηνται: perfect of κτάομαι ("acquire") with present sense "possess."
21.1 δεῖ: double construction: "there is need" + genitive; then, "it is necessary" + accusative + infinitive.
εἰ ξυστῶσιν: second aorist active (intransitive) subjunctive of ξυνίστημι. εἰ should be emended to ἤν; see D.
ἀντιπαράσχωσιν . . . ἱππικόν: i.e., ἀντιπαράσχωσιν ἱππικὸν ᾧ ἀμυνούμεθα (future).
2 αἰσχρόν: sc. ἐστι.
αὐτόθεν: "from here" (Athens).
ἐπιέναι: sc. δεῖ.
πολύ . . . αὐτῶν: "far from our own (land)."
ἐν τῷ ὁμοίῳ . . . καί: "in the same (situation) as"; see D.
τῇδε: "in this (land) here."
ἀπαρτήσοντες: "going to remove (ourselves)."
22.1 ἤν τινα . . . πεῖσαι: "if we can either persuade someone . . . ," i.e., "anyone . . . whom we can either persuade . . ."
καὶ πολύ: "even by much."
πολλὴ γὰρ . . . ὑποδέξασθαι: odd personal construction, easier to translate as impersonal; "it will not be (the part) of every city to receive it, since it is (so) large."
μὴ ἐπὶ ἑτέροις γίγνεσθαι: "not be dependent on others."
λόγῳ . . . μάλιστα: i.e., not in reality.
ἂν . . . εἶναι: infinitive in indirect discourse, for potential optative (S 1826).

23.1 ἀντίπαλον . . . παρασκευασάμενοι: sc. παρασκευήν.
οἷοί τε ἐσόμεθα: "we will be able."
2 πόλιν: object of οἰκιοῦντας (future participle of οἰκίζω, expressing purpose).
οὕς: refers not to preceding datives but to subject of οἰκιοῦντας ἰέναι.
κατάσχωσιν < κατέχω, here, "put in to land."
3 δέον: participle of δεῖ, in indirect discourse after εἰδώς.
πλείω = πλείονα, adverbial accusative.
ὅτι ἐλάχιστα = ὡς ἐλάχιστα (S 1086).
24.2 τὸ . . . ἐπιθυμοῦν: See on τῷ ἐμῷ διαπρεπεῖ, 16.2, and S 1153b N.2.
ἐξῃρέθησαν < ἐξαιρέω, "they did not have their eagerness taken away."
τοὐναντίον περιέστη αὐτῷ: "the opposite turned out for him (Nicias)," from what he expected.
δὴ καί: "surely also."
3 ὡς . . . σφαλεῖσαν μεγάλην δύναμιν: accusative absolute (S 2078), "on the grounds that . . ."
εὐέλπιδες ὄντες: grammatically free.
ὅμιλος καὶ στρατιώτης: either "the average citizen and soldier," or στρατιώτης is predicate with the following infinitives, "the masses expecting also (καί) to draw pay as a soldier."
οἴσειν, προσκτήσεσθαι: sc. εὐέλπιδες ὄντες.
4 ἡσυχίαν ἦγεν: "kept quiet."
25.1 οὐκ ἔφη: "he denied/said . . . not."
ψηφίσωνται: deliberative subjunctive (S 2677a), "should vote."
2 πλευστέα εἶναι: "they must sail" (S 1003a, 1052 for neuter plural).
κατὰ λόγον: "in proportion with (their) calculation(s)."
ἤν τι ἄλλο . . . δοκῇ: "anything else which seems"; see on ἤν τινα . . . πεῖσαι, 22.1.
26.1 αὐτοκράτορας εἶναι: subject is τοὺς στρατηγούς in next line.
πράσσειν: governed by ἐψηφίσαντο.
2 αὐτόθεν: from Athens.
ἀνειλήφει: pluperfect of ἀναλαμβάνω.
ἔς . . . ἡλικίας . . . ἐπιγεγενημένης: "with respect to the number of the new (ἐπι-) generation which had grown up."
27.1 πρόσωπα: accusative of respect with aorist passive περιεκόπησαν, "had their faces mutilated."

2 ᾔδει < οἶδα.
δημοσίᾳ: "at public expense"; with μηνύτροις.
οὗτοι: refers to τοὺς δράσαντας.
ἐψηφίσαντο: subject is the Athenians.
εἴ τις ... οἶδεν: "anyone who knew any other ..."
ἀδεῶς: i.e., without fear of countersuit, "with impunity"; see D.
3 μειζόνως: intensive comparative, "seriously."
ἐπὶ ... πραγμάτων: "with a revolutionary conspiracy in mind."
28.1 τὰ μυστήρια: the Eleusinian mysteries.
ἐπῃτιῶντο < ἐπαιτιάομαι, "blame x (accusative) for y (genitive), accuse x of y."
2 αὐτά: the charges against Alcibiades; object of ἐμεγάλυνον in lines 8-9, as well as of ὑπολαμβάνοντες.
μή ... προεστάναι: with ἐμποδὼν ὄντι, "being (since he was) in the way of themselves (σφίσιν αὐτοῖς) being leaders."
The μή is redundant.
ἐπιλέγοντες τεκμήρια: "adding on as proof."
29.1 εἴ τι: explains κρίνεσθαι; "to be judged, (as to) whether ..."
δίκην δοῦναι: "pay the penalty"; governed by ἑτοῖμος ἦν.
2 ἐπεμαρτύρετο: "conjured, invoked"; followed by two different constructions: infinitives μή ... ἀποδέχεσθαι and ἀποκτείνειν, and ὅτι clause.
ἀπόντος: "when he was not present"; early placement in prepositional phrase is emphatic.
ἐπί: "over, in command of."
3 θεραπεύων ὅτι: "protecting (his interests), because ..." (D).
ἐνιέντες < ἐνίημι.
ἐκ μείζονος διαβολῆς: "from a position of greater prejudice."
μετάπεμπτον κομισθέντα: "returning under summons" (D).
ἔδοξε: standard opening of decrees; "it seemed (best)," i.e., "it was decreed, resolved."
30.1 τοῖς ... : datives with pluperfect εἴρητο, "the order had been given," in line 32.
ξυνείπετο < συνέπομαι.
Κέρκυραν: Corcyra, modern Corfu.
ὡς ... διαβαλοῦσιν: future participle expressing purpose.
Ἰόνιον: "the Ionian (Gulf)," between Greece and Italy.
εἴ τινες ... παρῆσαν: See on ἤν τι ἄλλο ... δοκῇ, 25.2.
ἅμα ἕῳ: "at dawn"; see on ἅμα ἦρι, 8.1.

Thucydides Book VI

- 2 ὡς εἰπεῖν: "so to speak."
 ὅσον πλοῦν: "how long/distant a voyage."
- 31.1 αὐτοὺς ἐσῄει: "came to them/into their minds."
 τῇ παρούσῃ ῥώμῃ... ἀνεθάρσουν: See D.
 κατὰ θέαν: "for/towards the spectacle."
 ἀξιόχρεων: masculine/feminine accusative singular of ἀξιόχρεως.
 τῶν: sc. παρασκευῶν.
- 2 καὶ ἡ αὐτή: sc. παρασκευή.
- 3 οὗτος δὲ ὁ στόλος: sc. ὡρμήθη.
 κατ' ἀμφότερα: explained by καὶ ναυσὶ καὶ πεζῷ following (D).
 ἐξαρτυθείς: See on ἐξήρτυται, 17.3.
 τὸ μὲν ναυτικόν: answered by τὸ δὲ πεζόν, next page line 3.
 τοῦ μὲν ... παρασχόντος: genitive absolute, answered by τῶν <δὲ> ... χρησαμένων in lines 30-32.
 ταύταις: refers to ναῦς in line 28.
- 4 πρός τε σφᾶς αὐτούς: answered by καὶ ἐς τοὺς ἄλλους Ἕλληνας in lines 6-7.
 ᾧ... προσετάχθη: "(rivalry) in that to which each one was assigned."
- 5 εἰ γάρ τις ἐλογίσατο: protasis of a long contrary to fact condition; the apodosis begins in line 16 with πολλὰ ἄν.
 ἃ ... ἀπέστελλε: "what it sent its generals with" (lit., "having").
 ἀνηλώκει: pluperfect of ἀναλίσκω.
 πάντα τινά: "every one."
 ἐφόδιον: "(as) travelling money."
 ἐπὶ μεταβολῇ: "for trade" (D).
 τὰ πάντα: "in all."
- 6 θάμβει, λαμπρότητι: datives of cause (S 1517) with περιβόητος ἐγένετο.
 στρατιᾶς ... ὑπερβολῇ: See D.
- 32.1 ὑπεσημάνθη < ὑποσημαίνω.
 νομιζομένας: "customary."
 κατὰ ναῦν ἑκάστην: "ship by ship," i.e., separately.
- 2 ἐπὶ κέρως: Attic contraction of κέραος, genitive sing. of κέρας; "in column/single file."
 τὸ πρῶτον: adverbial, "at first."
 ἠπείγοντο < ἐπείγω; passive = "hasten (oneself)."
- 33.1 τὰ μὴ ... εἶναι: "things which seem not to be credible."
 καταφοβηθεὶς ἐπισχήσω: "hold back out of fear."

λέγειν: with πείθων ἐμαυτόν, "being convinced."
2 ξυμμαχίᾳ: This and following datives are causal, "because of/for the purpose of . . ."
3 ὡς . . . παρεσομένων: genitive absolute, "on the grounds that they will soon be here."
ὁρᾶτε: imperative.
ὅτῳ = ᾧ τινι.
4 ἐκπλαγῇ: aorist passive subjunctive of ἐκπλήσσω ("be amazed at"), expressing negative prohibition.
οἷοί τ' ἔσονται: See on 23.1.
ἀνωφελεῖς: "harmful, to our disadvantage"; sc. εἰσι.
ἀπώσωμεν: aorist subjunctive of ἀπωθέω, "repel, drive back."
οὐ . . . μὴ τύχωσι . . . φοβοῦμαι: Verbs of fearing always require μή (the negative is μὴ οὐ), "I do not fear they may obtain the things which they expect."
5 τῆς ἑαυτῶν: sc. γῆς; "their own land."
ἀπάραντες < ἀπαίρω, "lift off, depart, sail away."
πλείους = πλείονες, + genitive of comparison.
ὄνομα: object of καταλείπουσιν.
κἂν περὶ σφίσιν . . . πταίσωσιν: "even if they trip themselves up."
34.1 τά τε αὐτοῦ: "matters here."
τοὺς μὲν . . . τοῖς δέ: "some . . . others."
2 διὰ φόβου: "in fear."
ὥστε . . . ἐθελήσειαν: "so that perhaps, . . . , they would be willing."
ταχ' ἂν . . . εἶναι: indirect discourse with νομίσαντες.
προήσονται < προΐημι, in a future most vivid protasis; "if they abandon/neglect Sicily (τάδε) . . ."
βουληθέντες: "if they want to."
4 τὸ ξύνηθες ἥσυχον: "your habitual indolence" (Jowett).
ἥκιστ' . . . ὀξέως: "not at all swiftly."
Σικελιῶται . . . μεθ' ἡμῶν: "if we Sicilians were willing, all of us, or if not, as many as possible (ὅτι πλεῖστοι) along with us (Syracusans)."
μετὰ . . . τροφῆς: "with two months' provisions."
δῆλον ποιῆσαι: like ἀπαντῆσαι governed by ἐθέλοιμεν.
τοῦ . . . περαιωθῆναι: articular infinitive; like τῆς Σικελίας, object of preposition περί.
μάλιστ' ἂν . . . ἐκπλήξαιμεν: apodosis of the future less vivid condition of which the protasis is εἰ ἐθέλοιμεν.

ἐς λογισμὸν καταστήσαιμεν: "make them reason."
ἂν εὐεπίθετος εἴη: "(their force) would be easily attacked"; < ἐπιτίθημι.
5 τῷ ... ἀθροωτέρῳ: "with a swift-sailing (force, which would be) more cohesive."
κεκμηκόσιν: "exhausted," < κάμνω, dative with ἐπιθοίμεθα.
ἔστι: "it *is* possible."
τὰ τῶν πόλεων ... ὑποδέξοιντο: prolepsis, "not being sure about the attitudes of the cities, (lit., "not having the [attitudes] of the cities secure,") whether they would receive them."
6 κατασκοπαῖς ... ὁπόσοι: "(finding out) by spying how many."
ἐξωσθῆναι ... χειμῶνα < ἐξωθέω; "be forced by the season into winter"; i.e., the long process of deliberation and intelligence-gathering will make the campaign drag on into winter.
τοῦ ἐμπειροτάτου ... λαβόντος: genitive absolute.
εἴ τι ... ὀφθείη: "if anything noteworthy from our side were seen," i.e., "if we were seen to do anything noteworthy."
7 ἀγγελλοίμεθα ... τὸ πλέον: See D.
εὖ οἶδ᾽ ὅτι: parenthetical, "(as) I well know."
τῶν δ᾽ ... ἵστανται: "men's opinions are fixed according to what is said."
8 οὐ ... ἐφθείρομεν: conative imperfect (S 1895), "we were not trying to destroy."
9 ὅσον οὔπω: "all but."
35.1 τί ἂν δράσειαν αὐτούς: "what could (the Athenians) do to them."
ὅτι = ὅ τι, "which."
36.2 ἐπηλυγάζωνται: "shade, conceal."
δύνανται: here, "signify, mean."
4 οὐ γὰρ αὐτοὺς εἰκός: "for it is not likely that they ..."
ἐλάσσω = ἐλάσσονα.
37.1 ἐξήρτυται: See on 17.3.
τῆς νῦν ... ἐπιούσης: genitive of comparison depending on κρείσσω in line 6, "(than) the army which is now, as they claim, coming against (us)."
εἶναι: infinitive after ἡγοῦμαι in line 3.
οἷς: the army, now masculine plural in reference to the men in it; dative with ἀκολουθήσοντας.
εἰ μή: "except."

2 παρὰ τοσοῦτον γιγνώσκω: "by so much as I know"; see D.
μόλις ἂν ... οὐκ ἂν ... διαφθαρῆναι: "it seems to me that with difficulty would they not be destroyed," i.e., it seems likely that they would be destroyed. For repeated ἂν see on 18.6.
ὅμορον οἰκίσαντες: "having settled (it) next door."
ἦ πού γε: "especially, surely" ("how much more," Jowett).
στρατοπέδῳ: dative of cause, "by reason of their having a camp" (Jowett).
ἐκ νεῶν ἱδρυθέντι: "established from shipboard," i.e., just after landing.
ἐκ σκηνιδίων ... παρασκευῆς goes with (1) στρατοπέδῳ ἱδρυθέντι, "(a camp) made of tents and limited/minimal supplies," or (2) οὐκ ἐξιόντες, "not going out far (from the tents)."

38.2 βουλομένους: participial construction after ἐπίσταμαι, "I know that they want ..."
αὐτούς: "themselves."
καὶ κατορθώσωσιν: "they might actually/even succeed."
3 ἔστιν ὅτε: parenthetical, "there is (a time) when," i.e., "sometimes."
4 ὧν ἐγὼ ... γενέσθαι: ὧν with τι, "(things) of which I will try ... never to let any happen in our time." περιιδεῖν = "disregard, allow by oversight."
ὧν βούλονται: ὧν goes with κολάζων; "punishing ... for things which" (genitive of crime and accountability, S 1376).
προπείσεται: future of προπάσχω.
τὰ μὲν ... τὰ δέ ... τὰ δέ: "in part ... in part ... in part."
5 ἐκ τοῦ ... ὑμᾶς: "because you were not competent."
μᾶλλον ἤ: "and not" (D).
ἰσονομεῖσθαι: governed by βούλεσθε in line 12.

39.1 καὶ ἄρχειν ἄριστα βελτίστους: "are also best at ruling in the best way."
2 ἀφελομένη ἔχει: "takes away and keeps."
σπεύδοντες: indirect discourse after μανθάνετε.

40.1 τοῦτο: "in this way" (D).
οἱ ἀγαθοί: though subject of infinitive, in the nominative as part of the main subject.
ὡς πρός: "on the grounds that they are addressed to."
ἀπαλλάγητε: aorist passive imperative of ἀπαλλάσσω, "cease from."

Thucydides Book VI

- 2 ἑλομένη ... ἄρχοντας: "having chosen you as leaders."
  αὐτὴ ... αὐτῆς: "(the city) itself by itself."
  ἐκ δὲ ... ἐπιτρέπειν: "by being on guard (and) not yielding (to you)."
- 41.3–4 οὐδεμία βλαβὴ τοῦ ... κοσμηθῆναι ... καὶ τῶν ... διαπομπῶν: "there is no harm in ..."
  - 4 ἐπιμέλειαν καὶ ἐξέτασιν: "audit and review."
- 42.1 ἔμελλον: "about to" takes future (ὁρμιεῖσθαι) and present (στρατοπεδεύεσθαι) infinitive (S 1959).
  καταγωγαῖς: "during their stopovers, when they landed."
  ῥᾴους = ῥᾴονες, comparative of ῥᾴδιος.
  κατὰ τέλη: "by divisions."
  - 2 εἰσομένας: See on σκεψομένους, εἰσομένους, 6.3.
- 44.1 πολλὰ ... καὶ ἄλλα: "many other (ships)" (S 2879).
  - 2 προσβαλοῦσα: "having made land."
  οὐδὲ τούτοις: "not even with these."
  - 3 οὗ: "where."
  παρεῖχον: subject is the people of Rhegion.
  οὐδὲ μεθ' ἑτέρων: "not on (with) either side."
  - 4 προσοίσονται < προσφέρομαι, "approach, deal with."
  τὰς προπλους ναῦς ἐκ τῆς Ἐγέστης: sc., "to return."
- 45.1 ὡς ἐπὶ τούτοις: "on these grounds/this basis."
  περιπόλια: "guardhouses."
  ὅσον οὐ: See on 34.9.
- 46.2 ἀντεκεκρούκει < ἀντικρούω, "be a hindrance."
  ἤρξαντο πείθειν: "began their persuasive efforts."
  σφίσιν: i.e., the Athenians.
  τῷ μὲν Νικίᾳ ... ἀλογώτερα: unusual personal construction, and intensive comparative; "to Nikias the report of the Segestans was expected, but to the other two it was even (quite) inexplicable."
  - 3 φιάλας ... οἰνοχόας ... θυμιατήρια: "shallow bowls, wine pitchers, incense burners."
  πολλῷ πλείω τὴν ὄψιν: "an appearance (that was) much greater."
  δυνάμεως: here, "value, quantity."
  ὡς οἰκεῖα ἕκαστοι: "as their own."
  - 4 ὡς ... πολύ: "for the most part."
  ἴδοιεν: optative in indirect discourse.
- 47.1 πρὸς ταῦτα: "accordingly."
  ᾐτήσαντο: sc. the Segestans, to whom αὐτούς and αὐτοῖς also refer.

ἀξιοῦν: "demand."
παραμείναντας: sc. the Athenians, subject of διαλλάξαι.
δι' ὀλίγου . . . ἀδοκήτου: "in a short time and unexpectedly."
οἷοί τε ὦσιν: See on 23.1.
προσαγαγέσθαι: "bring over to their (the Athenians') side."
τῇ πόλει . . . κινδυνεύειν: See on τοῖς ἑτοίμοις, 9.3.
τὰ οἰκεῖα: "their own resources."

48.1 τοὺς μὲν ἀφιστάναι: transitive, "make some (cities) stand away, separate them."
τοὺς δὲ φίλους ποιεῖσθαι: middle, "make others friendly (to themselves)."
Μεσσηνίους: the people of Messana, modern Messina, on the straits between Italy and Sicily.
προσβολῇ: here, "approach."
οἱ μέν . . . οἱ δέ: "the latter . . . , the former."
ἐῶσι < ἐάω.

49.2 τὸ . . . πρῶτον: "at first."
τῇ ὄψει: "at the sight (of it)."
σφεῖς: The reflexive is used to contrast main subject of indirect discourse (the Athenians) with subject of προσδέχονται (the Syracusans) (S 1228b N.1). It is nominative because it includes Lamachus, the subject of ἔφη.

3 ἀποληφθῆναι < ἀπολαμβάνω, "cut off."
μὴ ἥξειν: redundant negative after verb of negative meaning (S 2739-2740).
ἐσκομιζομένων αὐτῶν: "while they (the Syracusans) were bringing (their property) in (to the city)."
οὔτε . . . ὁδόν: i.e., not far either by sea or by land.

50.3 τὰ Συρακοσίων βουλόμενοι: "partisans of Syracuse" (D).
4 ἐπὶ κέρως: See on 32.2.
Λεοντίνους . . . κατοικιοῦντες: "to resettle the Leontinians in their own (land)."
ἀδεῶς: See on 27.2.
ἀπιέναι: future in sense; the construction has shifted to indirect discourse.

5 ἐξ ἧς . . . ἦν: "(the land) setting out from which (i.e., with which as a base) they had to fight."

51.1 τετραμμένων: "paying attention to," < τρέπω.
κακῶς: with ἐνῳκοδομημένην, "blocked."
διελόντες < διαιρέω.

Thucydides Book VI

52.1 προσχωροῖεν ἄν: i.e., "they (the Kamarinaians) would go over to them."
ἐπὶ Καμαρίνης: "for (i.e., towards) Kamarina."
σχόντες ἐς: "having put in at" (LSJ A.II.8).
2 κατά τι: "at some (part)."
53.1 ὡς κελεύσοντας: For plural, see on οἷς, 37.1.
τῶν . . . μεμηνυμένων: partitive genitive; "(soldiers of the group) of those accused with him."
περὶ τῶν μυστηρίων: "(some) in connection with the mysteries."
2 πάντα ὑπόπτως ἀπο δεχόμενοι: "receiving everything with suspicion" (contra D); similar phrase in 53.3.
πίστιν: "trust/belief in" + genitive of person.
τινὰ . . . διαφυγεῖν: "for someone, even one seeming to be upright, to get off without being questioned once he was accused."
3 χαλεπὴν . . . γενομένην: accusative + infinitive after ἐπιστάμενος. τελευτῶσαν is used adverbially, "became harsh in the end."
54.1 ἀποφανῶ: future.
2 ὥρᾳ ἡλικίας: dative of respect or cause, "in the bloom of his youth."
μέσος πολίτης: "a citizen of middle rank."
3 ὡς . . . ἀξιώσεως: "as far as his standing permitted" (D); ὡς restrictive (S 2993).
4 οὐδὲν μᾶλλον: sc. than before.
ὡς οὐ διὰ τοῦτο: "as though not on this account."
προπηλακιῶν: contract future of προπηλακίζω, "bespatter with mud, smear."
5 τὴν ἄλλην ἀρχήν: "in the rest of his administration."
τύραννοι οὗτοι: "these, as tyrants"; see D.
Ἀθηναίους . . . πρασσόμενοι: "exacting from the Athenians."
τῶν γιγνομένων: "produce."
6 αὐτὴ ἡ πόλις . . . ἐχρῆτο: "the city observed by itself," i.e., "without interference" (D).
κειμένοις: "laid down"; κεῖμαι serves as passive to τίθημι.
πλὴν . . . εἶναι: "except insofar as they always took care that one of themselves should be in office."
ἦρξαν . . . ἀρχήν: "held the eponymous archonship in Athens" (D).
ἄρχων: participle, "while in office."

7 ἧς: "his," < ὅς, ἥ, ὅν.
55.1 αὐτῷ τούτῳ: "by this very thing."
3 οὐ μὴν οὐδ᾽: "and again, not . . ." (Denniston p. 339, s.v. μήν III.2 (ii).
διὰ τὸ . . . φοβερόν: "on account of the fear he customarily inspired before in the citizens"; see D's introduction, I.3.7-8.
πολλῷ . . . ἀσφαλοῦς: "by means of the abundance of his security, which was great (πολλῷ)."
ἐν ᾧ: "at a time when."
4 Ἱππάρχῳ δὲ ξυνέβη . . . προσλαβεῖν: "It happened to Hipparchus that" + indirect discourse, with shift from dative to accusative ὀνομασθέντα; καί = "also."
ἐς τὰ ἔπειτα: "for the future, in time to come."
56.1 οἴσουσαν < φέρω.
τὴν ἀρχήν: adverbial.
2 αὐτοῖς: the usual dative of agent with (plu)perfect passive.
ξυνεπιθησομένους: "those going to join (συν-) in putting (τίθημι) a hand to (ἐπι-)."
ἐν ὅπλοις: with ἁθρόους γενέσθαι.
καὶ ἔδει . . . ἐκείνους: See D.
57.1 ὡς ἕκαστα: "how each (element) . . ."
2 ὅσον οὐκ: See on 34.9.
ἤδη: "immediately."
ξυλληφθήσεσθαι < συλλαμβάνω.
3 ὥσπερ εἶχον: "just as they were"; ἔχω + adverb = εἰμί + adjective.
ὡς ἂν . . . ὀργῆς: "as (men do) in extreme anger."
4 τὸ αὐτίκα: "for the moment."
διετέθη < διατίθημι, "dispose (of)."
αὐτοῦ: "there."
58.1 ἀδήλως . . . ξυμφοράν: See D.
2 εἴ τις ηὑρέθη: See on ἤν τι ἄλλο . . . , 25.2.
59.2 διὰ φόβον . . . ὤν: See on 34.2.
εἴ ποθεν . . . οἱ: "(to see) if he could see some safety from somewhere existing for him, if a revolution occurred."
3 μέγα παρὰ . . . δύνασθαι: "have great influence with."
τῶν ἐφ᾽ ἑαυτοῦ: "men of his own time."
νοῦν: accusative of respect with ἤρθη (< αἴρω).
4 Ἀλκμεωνιδῶν τῶν φευγόντων: "of the exiles, the Alkmeonids" (D).
ὡς βασιλέα: ὡς = πρός, only when the object is a person.

60.1 ὁ δῆμος... ὑπόπτης: The words and thought echo those just preceding the digression on the tyrannicides; a loose form of ring composition.
2 καθ' ἡμέραν: "daily."
ἐπεδίδοσαν: intransitive, "advanced."
τὸ... ξυλλαμβάνειν: articular infinitive
ἐνταῦθα: "here, at this point," picking up ὡς ("when, as").
εἴτε ἄρα... καὶ οὔ: "to give information, whether actually (καί) true or even (καί) if not."
ἐπ' ἀμφότερα: "both ways."
οὐδεὶς... ἔχει εἰπεῖν: See on ἔχω, 2.1.
3 εἰ μὴ καὶ δέδρακεν: See D.
ὁμολογήσαντι: "if he confessed."
ἀρνηθέντι... ἐλθεῖν: "if he denied (the charge) and stood trial," a shift of construction paralleled in Thucydides.
4 τῶν... καταγνόντες: "having passed a sentence of death on those who had escaped."
5 κἂν τούτῳ: "and in this (matter)."
61.1 λόγου καὶ τῆς ξυνωμοσίας: explanatory καί, "purpose, that is of conspiracy."
2 ἐδόκει... ἥκειν: "it seemed that (the Spartans) were coming."
3 διαχρήσασθαι: "put to death."
4 περιειστήκει: pluperfect (intransitive) of περιίστημι.
ὧν πέρι ἄλλων = τοὺς ἄλλους περὶ ὧν (inverse attraction of antecedent to case of relative, S 2533); for accent of πέρι see on 16.1.
ἐμεμήνυτο: impersonal passive, "information had been received."
5 εἴρητο: See on τοῖς..., 30.1.
πεισθῆναι: subject is the Mantineans and the Argives, understood from previous clause.
6 ὡς: "as though."
ἐπὶ διαβολῇ: "in an atmosphere of prejudice."
7 ἐρήμῃ δίκῃ: "a trial in absentia."
62.1 ξύμπαντι: "with the whole (army)."
ἐπί... Ἐγέστης: See on ἐπὶ Καμαρίνης, 52.1.
2 ἔσχον ἐς: See on σχόντες ἐς, 52.1.
4 τἆλλα χρηματίσας: "having done (his) other business."
τάλαντα: subject of ἐγένοντο ("came"); see on ἐλάχιστα, 13.1.

5 τοὺς τῶν Σικελῶν ξυμμάχους: "their allies among the Sikels" (D).
63.1 ὡς ... ἰόντες: purpose.
2 πρός: "in accordance with."
κατά τε ... ἀνεθάρσουν: coordinated with the other main verbs κατεφρόνησαν and ἠξιοῦν by καί (line 25).
τὰ ἐπ᾽ ἐκεῖνα = τὰ ἐπέκεινα, "the far side" of Sicily.
φιλεῖ: "is wont/apt" + infinitive.
3 ἄλλα τε καὶ εἰ ξυνοικήσοντες ... : See D.
64.1 ἐν τοσούτῳ: "in the meantime."
καταλαμβάνειν: governed by βουλόμενοι in line 3.
ἐν ἐπιτηδείῳ: "in an advantageous (position)."
ὁμοίως ... καί: "the same as" (D).
ψιλούς, ὄχλον: Athenians; objects of βλάπτειν in line 10.
τῶν Συρακοσίων: with τοὺς ἱππέας, subject of βλάπτειν (D).
σφίσι ... ἱππέων: "since their own cavalry were not present."
οὕτω δέ: i.e., by the plan described before the parenthesis.
λήψεσθαι < λαμβάνω; subject is the Athenians.
βλάψονται: future middle used as passive.
τῷ Ὀλυμπιείῳ: See D on 65.3.
3 τοὺς παρὰ σφίσι: "those (troops) with them," i.e., inside the city.
τὸ στράτευμα: object of αἱρήσειν.
65.1 μετὰ τοῦ ... θαρσεῖν: "along with being confident in other respects also."
παρεσκευάσθαι: perfect middle, therefore "be prepared," not "make preparations." Hence the awkwardness of D's alternative (a), removable by deleting παρεσκευάσθαι (as D suggests), or by emending to παρασκευάσασθαι ("be planning ... to make preparations to go").
3 ἀνῆκται < ἀνάγω.
ἐβοήθουν ... πόλιν: "went to the city to help."
66.1 ἔμελλον: "were likely to."
λυπήσειν: future infinitive with understood optative of μέλλω (hence ἄν), supplied from ἔμελλον in line 16.
2 κατενεγκόντες < καταφέρω.
ἔρυμά τι: See D.
λογάδην: "picked, chosen."
διὰ ταχέων = ταχέως.
67.1 ἐπὶ ὀκτώ: "eight deep" (file), not "eight abreast" (rank).
εὐναῖς: i.e., tents.

Thucydides Book VI

- 2 ὅσον, ὡς: with numbers, "about."
  παρὰ δ' αὐτούς: "beside them, on their flank."
- 68.1 παραινέσει: dative with χρῆσθαι.
- 2 ὑπομενοῦσι: future.
  ἥσσω ἔχειν: See on ὥσπερ εἶχον, 57.3.
- 3 παραστήτω: 3rd singular aorist imperative of παρίστημι.
  εὖ οἶδ' ὅτι: See on 34.7.
  οὐκ ἐν πατρίδι ... ἀποχωρεῖν: See D.
- 4 τῶν πολεμίων: genitive of comparison.
- 69.1 στρατόπεδον: "army."
  ἀπροσδόκητοι: here, "not expecting" (D).
  καθίσταντο: because all "took their stand," though individually (ἕκαστος).
  τῷ ... ἐλλείποντι αὐτῆς: "on account of the lack of it (knowledge)."
  ὅμως: "nonetheless"; with ἀντεπῆσαν.
- 2 τροπὰς ... ἐποίουν: "made routs of one another such as (it is) likely for light troops (to make)."
- 3 τῆς ἰδίας ... ἐλευθερίας: "each man for his immediate preservation and future freedom."
  οἰκείαν σχεῖν: "to get (it) as their own"; epexegetic (explanatory) to ἀλλοτρίας (γῆς).
  ξυγκτήσασθαι ... ἦλθον: "to acquire along with them (the Athenians) the things for which they came."
  περὶ τῆς αὐτίκα ... κρατῶσι: See D.
- 70.1 ἐν χερσί: "hand to hand, at close quarters."
  ξυνεπιλαβέσθαι: "contribute to" + genitive.
- 2 ὠσαμένων: aorist middle participle of ὠθέω.
  παρερρήγνυτο: "was breached," of a line of battle.
- 3 ἀνέστελλον < ἀναστέλλω, "repulse."
  ἀσφαλῶς εἶχε: "was safe."
- 4 ὡς ἐκ τῶν παρόντων: See on ὡς ... ἀξιώσεως, 54.3.
- 71.2 πρίν: governs all the subjunctives in the sentence, except for ἱπποκρατῶνται (governed by ὅπως μή).
  ὅσων δέοι: "however much else there was need of."
- 72.3 ὡς εἰπεῖν: See on 30.2.
- 4 ὅπως ... ἔσονται: See on ἔπεισι, 18.2.
  ὡς πλεῖστοι: See on ὡς πλεῖστα, 14.1.
  τῇ ἄλλῃ μελέτῃ: "general training."
  ἐπιδώσειν: here intransitive, "increase."
  ἑαυτῆς: genitive of comparison with θαρσαλεωτέραν.
- 5 ἦ μήν: "in truth"; prefaces an oath (S 2865).

73.2 πείθωσι: object is Λακεδαιμονίους in next line.
αὐτούς: the Athenians.
74.1 ὡς προδοθησομένην: "(thinking) that it would be betrayed" (< προδίδωμι).
ἐπράσσετο: conative imperfect; subject is ἅ.
οἱ δὲ ... βουλόμενοι: See D.
75.1 Ἐτείχιζον: "built a wall," with cognate accusative τεῖχος; Here "walled, fortified," with object τὰ Μέγαρα.
ὁρῶν: neuter.
δι᾽ ἐλάσσονος: "at less distance."
φρούριον: "(as a) guardpost."
ἀποβάσεις: "points of disembarkation."
2 τῆς ... γῆς αὐτῶν: partitive genitive, "some of their land."
3 προσαγάγοιντο: optative in secondary sequence, for deliberative subjunctive.
76.1 καταπλαγῆτε: aorist passive subjunctive of καταπλήσσω; "be dismayed at."
3 τοὺς μὲν ... κατεστρέψαντο: See D.
4 οὗτοι: i.e., the Athenians.
περὶ δὲ ... καταδουλώσεως: See D.
77.1 ἀποφανοῦντες ἐν εἰδόσιν: "to reveal among those who know."
ἔχοντες ... Ἑλλήνων: See D.
2 κατὰ πόλεις: "city by city."
ἐκπολεμοῦν: "to bring to war."
τοῖς δὲ ... κακουργεῖν: "and harm others as they can, (by) saying something attractive to each."
καὶ οἰόμεθα ... δυστυχεῖν: See D.
78.1 τὸν μὲν Συρακόσιον: sc. πολέμιον ὄντα (the following οὐ need not be accented).
ἀγωνιεῖται: contract future of ἀγωνίζομαι.
κολάσασθαι, βεβαιώσασθαι: governed by βούλεσθαι.
3 προεμένῳ: "for (him) having abandoned (me)" (D).
τοὺς αὐτοὺς κινδύνους: object of προσλαβεῖν.
4 τὰ δεύτερα κινδυνεύσοντας: "next in line to run risks."
αὐτούς: "yourselves," i.e., "of your own accord."
ἅπερ ... ἐπεκαλεῖσθε: "the very things asking for which you would have appealed to (us)."
φαίνεσθαι: governed by εἰκὸς ἦν ὑμᾶς in line 4.
79.1 θεραπεύσετε: "will have concern for."
καὶ τοῖς ... βοηθεῖν: "and (you agreed) to help the Athenians."

ὑπ' ἄλλων: sc. ἀδικῶνται (D).
2 τοῦ καλοῦ δικαιώματος: "the specious claim" (D).
80.1 Πελοπόννησον ... οἵ: See on οἷς, 37.1.
ἴσην: "fair."
τὸ μηδετέροις ... βοηθεῖν: explains προμηθίαν.
ὡς καί: "as in fact."
2 σωθῆναι: epexegetic, or natural result without ὥστε.
3 ἐκδιδάσκειν: depends on οὐδὲν ἔργον εἶναι.
4 τῆς αἰτίας: genitive of crime and accountability with τιμωρίαν (S 1375).
5 κἂν περιγενόμενοι ... διαφυγεῖν: See D.
82.2 ἔχει δὲ καὶ οὕτως: "and that is indeed the case" (D).
Ἴωνες ὄντες Πελοποννησίοις: sc. πολέμιοι, contra D.
3 οὐδὲν προσῆκον μᾶλλόν τι: accusative absolute, "it being not at all more fitting."
οἰκοῦμεν: "we govern (them)."
ἐς τὸ ἀκριβὲς εἰπεῖν: "strictly speaking."
4 ἐβούλοντο: governs both δουλείαν and ἐπενεγκεῖν; see D.
83.2 καλλιεπούμεθα < καλλιεπέομαι, "say in elaborate language."
3 ἐπὶ τὸ φοβερώτερον: "rather over-fearfully."
4 οὐ δουλωσόμενοι: sc. ὑμᾶς (D).
84.1 διὰ τὸ ... ἀντέχειν: "because you, being not weak, hold out against the Syracusans."
3 ὅτι μάλιστα: "as much as possible."
85.2 παροκωχῇ: "provision, supplying."
βιαιότερον: "on harsher terms."
3 ὥστε καὶ τἀνθάδε ... καθίστασθαι: See D.
ἀρχῆς ... ὑμῶν: "they are eager to rule you."
τῷ ἡμετέρῳ ... ὑπόπτῳ: "suspicion of us."
ἀνάγκη δέ: sc. that the Syracusans will rule Sicily.
86.1 προσείοντες: "brandishing (as a menace)."
3 μὴ μεθ' ὑμῶν: "except with you."
4 ἄλλα, τά: accusative of respect.
τολμῶσιν ἐπὶ ... παρακαλεῖν ὑμᾶς: "they dare to appeal to you against ..."
5 παρασχήσειν: here, impersonal with ὑμῖν, "be in your power."
πολλοστὸν μόριον: "a small fraction."
περανεῖ: contract future of περαίνω.
87.2 ξύμμαχοι ... ἥκειν: dependent on φαμέν, "we claim that we come as allies."

3 ἡμῖν: rare use of dative of agent with present passive (S 1490).
τὸ αὐτό: "at the same time."
4 πᾶς: amplified by ὅ τε οἰόμενος . . . καὶ ὁ ἐπιβουλεύων, then resumed with plural ἀμφότεροι.
διὰ τὸ ἑτοίμην . . . κινδυνεύειν: See D.
88.3 ὅπως: clause of purpose, not effort (for the distinction see S 2208).
4 οἱ πολλοὶ ἀφειστήκεσαν: See D.
καὶ πρότερον: "even before (the Athenians arrived)."
εἰσὶν οἵ: See on 10.3.
5 ἀπεκωλύοντο: sc. προσαναγκάζειν; see D's introduction, I.3.18.
6 εἰ δύναιντο: "(to see) if they would be able."
ἔστιν ὧν: genitive (absolute) of ἔστιν αἵ.
πλινθία: See D.
σίδηρον: "iron" for clamping wall blocks together.
ὡς . . . ἑξόμενοι: "with the intention of taking (the war) in hand" + genitive.
ἅμα τῷ ἦρι: See on 8.1.
8 ὥστε . . . ἀμύνειν: result clause, after a verb (ψηφισάμενοι) which more commonly takes an infinitive without ὥστε (S 2271).
αὐτοῖς: the Syracusan ambassadors.
αὐτοῦ: "there," i.e., in Greece.
10 ξυνέβη: "it happened that (there were) . . ."
τὰ αὐτὰ . . . δεομένους: "making the same requests as Alcibiades."
μὴ ξυμβαίνειν: See on μὴ ἥξειν, 49.3.
89.1 τῆς ἐμῆς διαβολῆς: "the slander against me."
τὰ κοινά: "public matters, matters of common interest."
2 πρὸς Ἀθηναίους καταλλασσόμενοι: "when you were reconciled/made peace with the Athenians."
δύναμιν, ἀτιμίαν: objects of περιέθετε.
4 ξυμπαρέμεινεν . . . ἡμῖν: "remained with us"; i.e., "we continued to . . ."
τοῖς παροῦσιν: "the prevailing (customs, conditions)."
6 δικαιοῦντες ἐν ᾧ σχήματι . . . τοῦτο ξυνδιασῴζειν: "thinking it right to join in saving that (form) in which . . ."
οὐδενὸς ἂν χεῖρον: i.e., better than anyone.
λέγοιτο: "could be said."
90.1 ἐμοί: dative of agent with impersonal ἐσηγητέον.

Thucydides Book VI

2 αὐτῶν: "themselves," as distinct from the ἀρχή.
3 ἤδη: "directly, immediately."
ἐντειχισάμενοι: "having walled in," i.e., blockaded."
4 εὐπορώτερον γίγνεσθαι: "be/become better provided for."
91.1 παρὰ τοῦ ... διενοήθημεν: "from the one who knows most exactly what we had in mind."
2 ξυστραφέντες: aorist passive participle of ξυστρέφω (συν + στρέφω).
καὶ νῦν: "even now."
3 ὃν ... κίνδυνον: "the danger which ..."
οὐκ: with διὰ μακροῦ.
4 ὥστε: "therefore."
ποιήσετε, πέμψετε: with εἰ, future most vivid protasis (S 2328).
στρατιὰν ... τοιαύτην ... οἵτινες αὐτερέται κομισθέντες: "this sort of army, men who having travelled as self-rowers ..."
καὶ ὃ ... νομίζω: "and, what I think is even more useful than the army."
ἄνδρα: object of πέμψετε in line 9, with ἄρχοντα in apposition, "as leader."
ὡς = ἵνα.
6 αὐτοῦ: genitive with διαπεπειρᾶσθαι.
εἰ ἃ μάλιστα ... ἐπιφέροι: See D.
ἐπισταμένους φοβεῖσθαι: "know and fear."
7 ἃ ... κωλύσετε: "the ways in which (ἃ, accusative of respect) ... while deriving benefit yourselves, you will hinder the opposition."
παρείς: aorist active participle of παρίημι.
δικαστηρίων: The Corinthians complain that Athens benefits unfairly by being the site of the international court (contra D).
92.1 ἐν ὑμῖν ἐστίν: "is in your hands, up to you."
γνώμης: genitive with ἁμαρτήσεσθαι.
2 τῇ ἐμαυτοῦ: "my own (city)"; dative with ἐπέρχομαι.
ὑποπτεύεσθαι: governed by ἀξιῶ in line 5; subject is τὸν λόγον.
ἐς τὴν φυγαδικὴν προθυμίαν: "with regard to the usual zeal of exiles" (see D).
3 τῆς ... πονηρίας, τῆς ... ὠφελίας: genitives of cause (S 1405); the latter perhaps genitive of purpose (S 1408).
4 τό τε φιλόπολι ... ἐπολιτεύθην: See D.
ἀπολέσας: "having lost."

5 ἐμοί: dative with χρῆσθαι in line 19.
γνόντας... λόγον: "recognizing this argument which is put forward by all."
ἤκαζον: "I was (only) guessing at."
τῶν διαφερόντων: "(your) vital interests."
μὴ ἀποκνεῖν: governed by ἀξιῶ in line 17; subject is αὐτούς in line 22, "(you) yourselves."
93.1 καὶ... πρότερον: "even before (Alcibiades spoke)."
2 καὶ τὸ παραυτίκα καί: "and immediately also."
3 οἱ πέμπειν: "to send to him (Gylippus)."
94.1 ἐπὶ Γέλωνος: "in the time of Gelon" (483 B.C.); see 4.1-2 and D on 4.2 and 2-5 (p. 2).
95.1 ἐπράθη < πιπράσκω.
2 οὐ κατέσχεν: "did not achieve its purpose" (D).
96.1 δυνηθῆναι: sc. ἀναβῆναι.
2 ἐξήρτηται: "is hung," i.e., is steep (D).
ἐπιπολῆς: preposition with τοῦ ἄλλου, "above the rest (of the place)."
3 παρειληφότες: perfect active participle of παραλαμβάνω.
97.1 χερσόνησος: "peninsula."
οὔτε... ὁδόν: See on 49.4.
3 ὡς ἕκαστος τάχους εἶχε: lit., "as each man had of speed," i.e., "each as fast as he could."
98.1 ἔλαβον: i.e., were given (D).
2 ἐπεξελθόντες... περιορᾶν: Subject is the Syracusans.
3 λιθοφορεῖν: The stones were for walls.
99.1 παρέβαλλον... αἰεί: "were forever (i.e., kept on) laying down."
2 καί εἰ... γίγνεσθαι: See D.
τρέπεσθαι: The subject is ἐκείνους πάντας.
3 ἐγκάρσιον: "at right angles" to the Athenian wall (D).
100.1 ὀχετοὺς... ποτοῦ ὕδατος: "drinking-water pipes"; see D.
ὑπονομηδόν: "underground."
εἰ ἐπιβοηθοῖεν: "in case (the enemy) should come to the rescue."
101.1 ταύτῃ: "in this (area)."
2 παρώρυσσον: "were digging alongside."
οἷόν τε ᾖ: impersonal, + dative.
3 τὸ πρὸς τὸν κρημνόν: sc. τεῖχος.
στεριφώτατον: "firmest."
αἱροῦσιν: historical present (cf. ἐπιχειροῦσιν in line 10), joined with εἷλον.

Thucydides Book VI

- 4 λογάδες: "picked, chosen."
- 5 ἦσαν . . . ἐνταῦθα: The parenthesis, to be taken with what follows, explains why they attacked.
  - ὁμόσε χωροῦσι: "come to close quarters with" + dative.
- 103.3 τοὺς δὲ λόγους . . . πρὸς τὸν Νικίαν: See D.
- 104.1 ἐπὶ τὸ αὐτό: "to the same (effect)."
  - περιποιῆσαι: "save."
  - τὸν Ἰόνιον: See on 30.1.
- 2 ἄρας < αἴρω, "set off."
  - ταύτῃ: "here."
  - κατὰ βορέαν ἑστηκώς: "rising in the North."
  - ἐς τὰ μάλιστα = μάλιστα.
- 105.2 ὅσον σχόντας . . . ἀπελθεῖν: "just to land . . . and go back."
  - ὅσα ἄλλα: See D.
  - εὐπροφάσιστον μᾶλλον: "more plausible."